Irish Alphabet

Irish Alphabet

By Rickey E. Pittman • Illustrated by Connie McLennan

PELICAN PUBLISHING COMPANY
Gretna 2011

"*Ce'ad mi'le fa'ilte*" (kaid meel-aa fall-cha)—"*One hundred thousand welcomes*"

To the Irish diaspora, wherever God has placed you.—R.E.P.

To Mary Viola Fennessey McLennan—C.M.

Library of Congress Cataloging-in-Publication Data

Pittman, Rickey.
  Irish alphabet / Rickey E. Pittman ; illustrated by Connie McLennan.
    p. cm.
  ISBN 978-1-58980-745-7 (hardcover : alk. paper) 1. Ireland—Juvenile literature.
 2. Alphabet books—Juvenile literature. I. McLennan, Connie. II. Title.
  DA906.P48 2011
  941.5—dc22

                              2010029020

Printed in Singapore
Published by Pelican Publishing Company, Inc.
1000 Burmaster Street, Gretna, Louisiana 70053

A is for the Aran Islands,
With their cold and wind-swept shores,
And for the abbeys in Armagh,
With their heavy, dark-oak doors.

B is for the Blarney Stone
And for great Brian Boru.
Beware the piercing banshee's cry
Or else she'll come for you!

C is for the Celtic Cross
You find in cemeteries.
Created by St. Patrick
As a mark for Christian sanctuaries.

D is for the faerie Dullahan,
A harbinger of death.
Riding a black steed,
He just may steal your breath.

E is for Erin, the Emerald Isle,
With it's forty shades of green.
I love to hear old Ireland's history
And see the pretty colleens.

F is for Finn MacCool,
A giant of a man.
He was Ireland's hero,
The strongest in the land.

G is for the Giant's Causeway,
Built by Finn MacCool.
He crossed it on a dare,
Defeating the challenging fool.

H is for the Irish harp
The Irish bards did play.
See it on its field of green
On Irish flags today.

I is for the Irish Brigade
Led by General Thomas Meagher.
With a cry, *"faugh a ballagh,"*
He was determined to win the war.

J is for James Joyce,
The famous Irish writer,
And also for the Irish jig
That makes our spirits brighter.

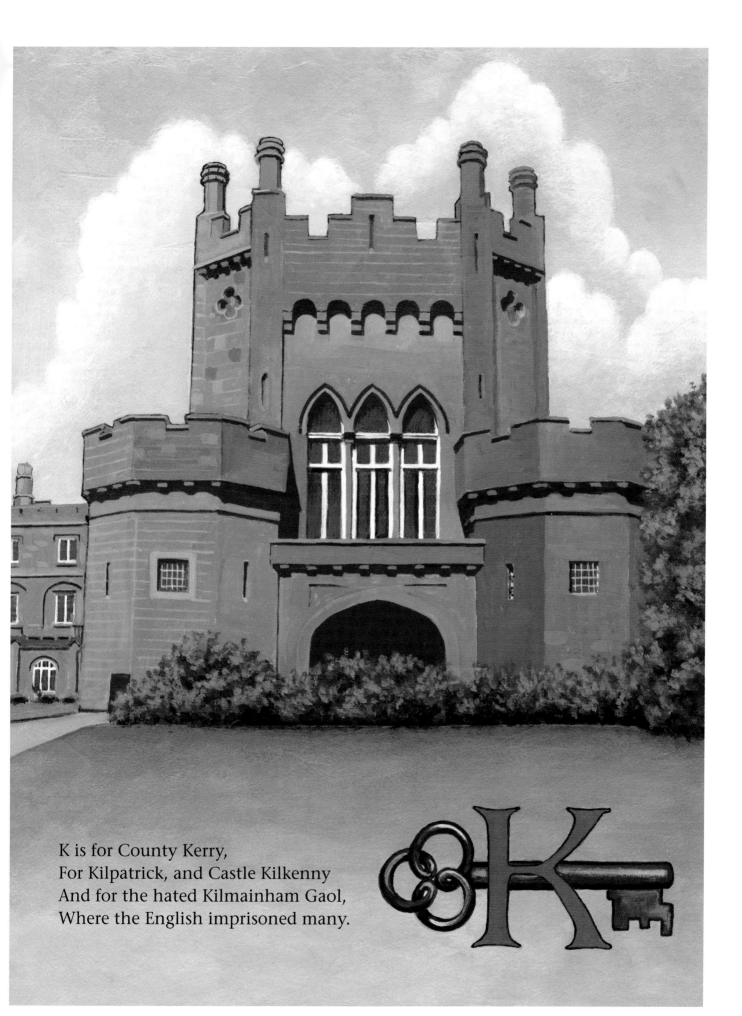

K is for County Kerry,
For Kilpatrick, and Castle Kilkenny
And for the hated Kilmainham Gaol,
Where the English imprisoned many.

L is for the little leprechauns
Who hide their crocks of gold.
Follow a rainbow's trail
For a sight you must behold.

M is for sweet Molly Malone.
She wheels her wheelbarrow
Through the long Dublin streets,
So broad and so narrow.

N is for mysterious Newgrange,
A passage-grave or tomb,
Where Cúchulainn was conceived,
In its dreamy, cold stone rooms.

O is for orange,
The color of King William.
He won the Battle of the Boyne
When King James failed to beat him.

P is for St. Patrick,
Who drove the snakes away.
He brought Ireland the
    Christian faith,
So we honor him today.

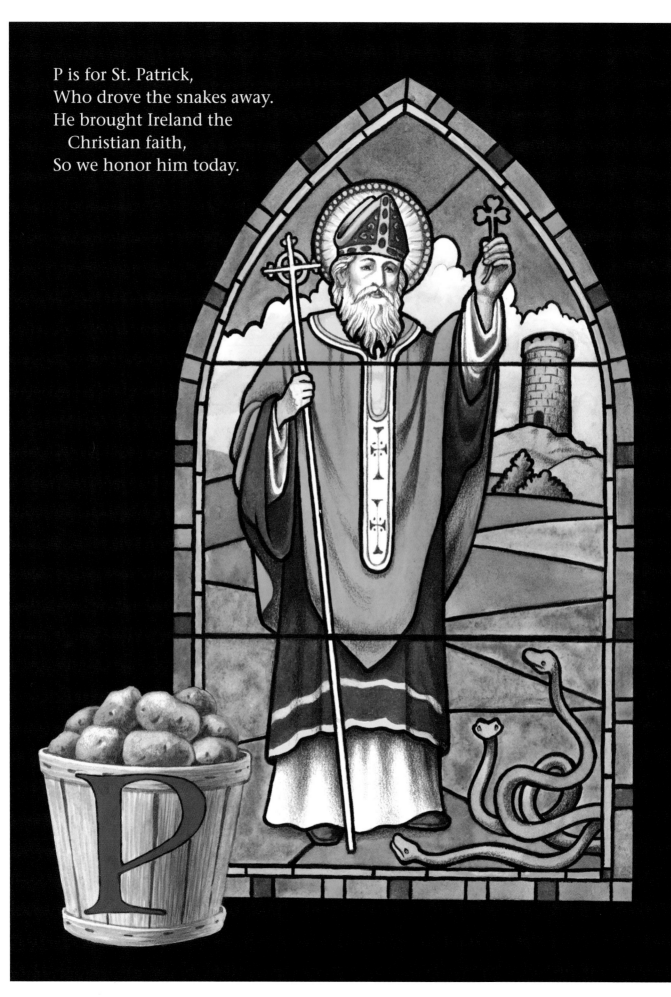

Q is for the Irish pirate queen;
Grace O'Malley was her name.
She captured many English ships,
And their treasures she did claim.

R is for the Rock of Dunamase,
Ancient fort that you should see.
And don't forget the Riverdancers
Whose feet flit with glee.

S is for the shamrock,
With three leaves for the Trinity,
And for the blackthorn walking cane
The Irish call the shillelagh.

T is for the three colors
On the Irish flag today
And for the tea the Irish drink;
We'll have some if you stay.

U is for the uilleann pipes,
With drones, chanter, and bellow.
The country's national bagpipe
Is a hit with Irish fellows.

V is for Vinegar Hill,
Where Irish rebels took a stand
Against the British forces,
Who had occupied their land.

W is for the Wolfhound,
Gentle giants they are called.
War-dog of the Celts,
Fierce and fast and tall!

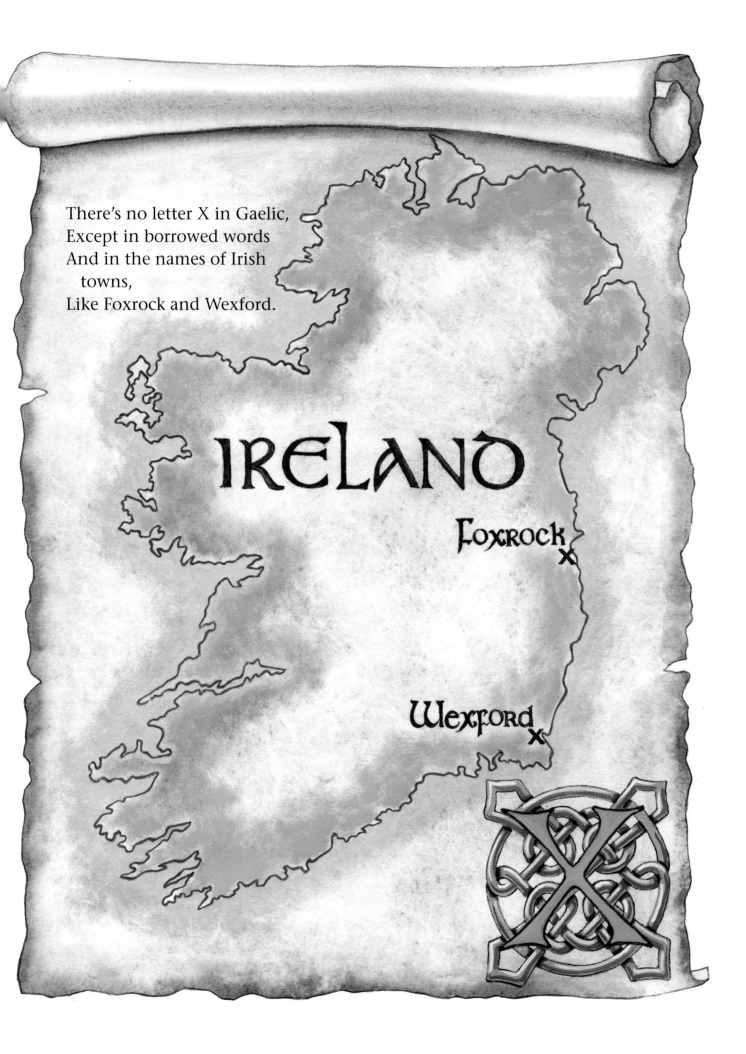

There's no letter X in Gaelic,
Except in borrowed words
And in the names of Irish
   towns,
Like Foxrock and Wexford.

IRELAND

Foxrock
×

Wexford
×

Y is for W. B. Yeats,
Who wrote poetry and plays.
He was Ireland's famous bard,
And we read him still today.

Z is for Zozimus—
Last gleeman of the Pale—
A composer of rhyming verse,
People loved to hear his tales.

Glossary

Brian Boru was able to match the Uí Néill. He defeated the Vikings in 999, and in 1002, he won recognition as king of all Ireland.

Kilmainham is pronounced *Kill-main-ahm*. Gaol is pronounced *jail*.

The Thirty-Two Counties of Ireland

Antrim	Limerick
Armagh	Londonderry
Carlow	Longford
Cavan	Louth
Clare	Mayo
Cork	Meath
Donegal	Monaghan
Down	Offaly
Dublin	Roscommon
Fermanagh	Sligo
Galway	Tipperary
Kerry	Tyrone
Kildare	Waterford
Kilkenny	Westmeath
Laois	Wexford
(pronounced *leesh*)	Wicklow
Leitrim	

Lyrics to "Molly Malone"

In Dublin's fair city,
Where the girls are so pretty,
I first set my eyes on sweet Molly Malone,
Who wheels her wheelbarrow
Through streets broad and narrow
Crying cockles and mussels alive, alive o!

Chorus
Alive, alive o! Alive, alive o!
Crying cockles and mussels alive, alive o!

She was a fishmonger
But sure 'twas no wonder
For so were her father and mother before
And they each wheeled their barrow
Through streets broad and narrow
Crying cockles and mussels alive, alive o!

Chorus

She died of a fever
And no one could save her
And that was the end of sweet Molly Malone
But her ghost wheels her barrow
Through streets broad and narrow
Crying cockles and mussels alive, alive o!